WALKS AROUND BRONTË COUNTRY

TEN WALKS OF SIX MILES OR UNDER

Colin Speakman

Dalesman

First published in 2010 by Dalesman
an imprint of
Country Publications Ltd
The Water Mill
Broughton Hall
Skipton
North Yorkshire BD23 3AG
www.dalesman.co.uk

Text © Colin Speakman 2010
Maps © Guelder Design & Mapping 2010
Illustrations © Christine Isherwood 2010

Cover: The Brontë Way at Top Withins by Mark Sunderland

ISBN 978-1-85568-272-6

Printed by Amadeus Press

Contents

Introduction

Those three remarkable sisters – Charlotte, Emily and Anne Brontë – who lived, worked and wrote in Haworth during the 1830s and '40s, transformed what had, until then, been a typical South Pennine industrial village, into a world famous literary shrine. The little Parsonage – now the Brontë Museum – the church (rebuilt since the Rev Patrick was there), the cobbled Main Street with the Black Bull Inn where Branwell drank himself to an early grave, but above all the wild Pennine moors that form such an evocative backcloth to the novels and poems, have attracted literary pilgrims from all over the world. Little wonder that the walk to the Brontë Falls or to Top Withins, the supposed setting of Wuthering Heights, is one of the few places in the UK where signposts are in Japanese.

But there is another Haworth, well away from the souvenir shops, cafes and antiques, a more workaday community on the outskirts of the busy town of Keighley. And, though the little steam railway no longer carries commuters from the villages of Oxenhope, Haworth and Oakworth to Keighley, it does bring weekend visitors on one of the most picturesque and frequently filmed heritage railways in the British Isles.

Beyond the busy villages is an older world of often ancient Pennine hill-farms, a wild countryside of desolate, open, even bleak, gritstone moorland, interspersed with deep, tree-lined, beck-filled gills of intense beauty.

This book explores all these different aspects of Haworth's countryside. Few areas of Britain have so many waymarked recreational paths – the Brontë Way, the Worth Way, the Railway Children's Path, the Millennium Way, the Aire-Calder Way, and even the Pennine Way, cut across the area. This makes choosing ten short walks around this area an easy task. All are accessible by excellent Keighley & District buses (with bargain K-Day and Metro Day Rover walkers' tickets available) and several can even be reached by steam train.

This is real hill country. Paths are often steep, usually muddy and stiles require agility – boots are essential most times of the year, and rainwear and emergency food and drink should always be carried. Have a good map – highly recommended is the OS Outdoor Leisure South Pennines map (OL21), or the excellent pocket-sized Haworth & District Stile Footpath Map with its hand-drawn paths, on sale in the Tourist Information Centre. Take all litter home with you, close gates (unless clearly propped open) and keep dogs on leads at all times – there are almost always sheep about.

Penistone Hill Country Park

Distance: 2½ miles (6km). Time: 1½ hours
Terrain: Moorland paths and tracks; two moderate climbs.
Start: Haworth Tourist Information Centre, grid ref 030373.
Parking: Choice of car parks in Haworth.
Refreshment/facilities: Excellent choice in Haworth; toilets near Parsonage.
Public Transport: Frequent buses 500, 664, 665 from Keighley (500 from
Hebden Bridge Station) plus Keighley Worth Valley trains to Haworth (adds
extra ¼ mile) at weekends and school holidays.

This short, fairly easy walk is designed to be combined with a stroll around Haworth and its famous cobbled Main Street, church and Parsonage, following old flagged paths out of the village to nearby Penistone Hill Country Park, which gives a real taste of the heather moors and wild landscapes that so inspired the Brontë sisters.

From Haworth Information Centre, walk a few yards down Main Street, but bear right before the Black Bull Inn, to take the flagged path through the metal kissing gate which leads below the church and through Haworth's melancholy graveyard, crowded with gravestones and overlooked by the gloomy Parsonage. Keep ahead on the flagged way, passing little allotments with hens, plus picnic areas and Bankfield car park.

At the crossing of paths, turn right following the Millennium Way signs to ascend the track, Balcony Lane, which climbs gently uphill, past former farm buildings at Balcony. At the lane, cross to a junction of paths at the entrance to Penistone Hill Country Park.

Penistone Hill Country Park is an area of splendid open countryside, 179 acres (72.5ha) of heather and rough grassy moorland just above Haworth village. There are splendid views from the summit over the Worth and Sladen Valleys, and to the crests of the South Pennine hills.

This is a wonderful area in which to stroll or picnic, but avoid the former quarry areas (much of the gritstone that built Haworth was quarried here) which can be dangerous.

Take the left of two signed paths towards Brontë Falls. This follow a moorland path gradually ascending. Ignore the first path that branches off, but take the second, also signed to the Falls, close to a single plank bridge over a streamlet. Follow this up to the moor summit, over a crossing path where directly ahead you'll see the white triangulation station (024367).

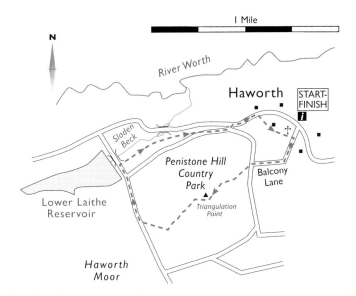

Though no longer required for navigation or mapping purposes, these OS measurement points make valuable landmarks. At 314 metres, or a little under 1,000 feet, and marking the highest point of the moor, the trig point offers a magnificent, panoramic viewpoint.

Your way is now along the narrow path, slightly to your right, which slopes north-westwards down the crest of the hillside to a much broader crossing path below. Turn left here, following the path as it winds its way below the former quarry workings with its heaps of discarded boulders.

Where a narrow path bears off right at a signpost (019364) follow it through the heather to the lane. Turn right, descending towards Lower Laithe Reservoir and the Sladen Valley. Keep ahead at the crossroads and along the pavement, ignoring the first path on the right opposite Intake Farm, but turn right (016367) just before the reservoir at the Waterworks entrance along a tarmac track to the right of the works. This climbs along the side of the Sladen Valley, with good views across, as your way becomes a gravel and grass track. This emerges on the lane by Haworth Cemetery. Go left here into Cemetery Road, soon picking up the path along the verge on the left which saves walking on the road – good views again from here.

At the crossroads keep straight ahead towards Haworth, but before the village look for a stone gap-stile and kissing-gate on the right which leads into a field with a flagged path. Follow this path over a couple of fields, and along a short enclosed way behind retirement homes to emerge at Haworth Parsonage and Museum. Straight ahead to the centre of the village.

Fieldhead & Haworth Brow

Distance: 4½ miles (7km). Time: 2½ hours
Terrain: Mainly field paths and lanes – one stretch of moorland. Two moderate climbs, but several stiles, some needing agility.
Start: Haworth Tourist Information Centre, grid ref 030373.
Parking: Choice of public car parks in Haworth.
Refreshment/facilities: Excellent choice in Haworth; toilets near Parsonage. Also at Oxenhope Station (when open). Picnic site at Oxenhope.
Public Transport: Bus 500, 663, 664 or 665, from Keighley. Keighley Worth Valley trains to Oakworth Station at weekends and school holidays.

A walk between Haworth and Oxenhope above the valley formed by the Bridgehouse Beck, returning through field paths climbing along the opposite side of the valley to cross Brow Moor and Haworth Brow. Enjoy spectacular views of Haworth in its industrial and moorland setting.

From the information centre, walk down the cobbled Main Street but bear right between the church and Black Bull Inn, through the iron kissing-gate and along the flagged path by the graveyard signed for Penistone Hill. Continue past allotments above the car park but keep directly ahead at the junction along the narrow enclosed paths signed to Oxenhope and waymarked the Brontë Way. After another 100 yards, this enclosed path between stone walls turns sharp right up towards Sowden Farm, then sharp left before the farm, alongside the stone wall along a field. Keep ahead at the little pedestrian gate at a crossing of paths. Where it reaches a tarmac lane (027366) bear right for 10 yards to rejoin the Brontë Way which now goes left alongside a cypress hedge behind the farm known as Hole. Keep the same direction through a gate and into a field, heading for stone steps in the wall corner into the next field below Field Head Farm still keeping the

Haworth

7

wall on your left. Look for a narrow gap ahead which leads into another short stretch of enclosed path into the next field. The wall is now on your right. Head through the gate ahead down towards the farm Old Oxenhope (029361) noting the mill pond on your right.

Turn left in the lane and descend to join Marsh Lane. Turn left here for 80 yards to where a track leads off on the right. This is Bents Lane, a stony track which descends the hillside. At Bents House keep ahead through the pedestrian gate on the left by a field gate, descending the side of the field towards the railway. Bear left at the stile down to the level crossing (checking to ensure no train is approaching) going over the footbridge over Bridgehouse Beck, then turn right to follow the path behind the sidings and carriage sheds to emerge at a track leading into Mill Lane just above Oxenhope Station.

Turn right here for the station for toilets and refreshments (on the right) or to enjoy the attractive Millennium Green picnic site on the left

The walk continues left up Mill Lane to the main A6033 Hebden Road. Cross with care. Almost opposite, to the left, is Dark Lane. A steady climb uphill leads to the white house, Little Haley (037352), to the immediate far side of which is a narrow way, signed Worth Way, alongside ivy-covered walls. Cross a stile into the field beyond, heading for Low Haley Farm. Go through the farm gate, but keep slightly right before the barn through the gate (038354) into a grassy track through another gate into the next field. Bear half right towards a stone gap-stile ahead (039355) following wall and hedge to a stile leading into the track past a farm entrance. Keep ahead towards the house known as Peat Cottage beyond and to the left of which a gate leads into a grassy track (042357). At the next gate turn sharp left (waymarked). This faint path climbs along a wall side and headland towards a plantation ahead. A stile leads into the track to Royd House Farm. Turn left here, but take the first gravel path right, which goes above another house and garden, waymarked, through little gates, finally, at the third gate, bearing sharp right to climb steeply through heather and a stile to reach the edge of Brow Moor. Turn left here onto Black Moor Road for 100 yards.

When you reach the open expanse of Brow Moor, look for the well-used path, right (041364), which ascends the moor, following a wall for some 300 yards to a small plantation opposite a gate (043365), where a narrow crossing path heads due north-westwards through the heather and rough grass.

The view from the crest of Haworth Brow is the highlight of the walk – a panoramic vista of the whole Worth Valley, an intermingling of the industrial and rural, the flat dark summits of the South Pennines an impressive backcloth.

Follow the path over and down the crest of the moor, soon bearing right.

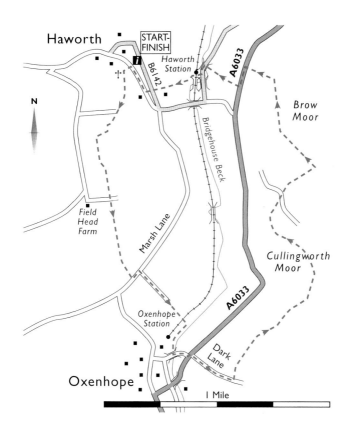

Where power lines cross at a small plantation (040370), take the path that forks left then twists sharply left, downhill, curving to meet a crossing path. Turn right here into Brow Top Road. Go left for some 50 yards to locate a path, right (039371), which leads in front of cottages before bearing left down a field to emerge at the A6033 by houses at a gate.

Go left for 100 yards to where, on the right, a tarmac path goes down steps leading into a housing estate. Keep straight ahead down Cliff Street. Left at the bottom into Prince Street, but look for an alleyway, right, which brings you into Mill Hey by the Royal Oak, just below Haworth Station and bus stops. Go over the railway footbridge, directly ahead up cobbled Butt Lane, over the pedestrian crossing across the bypass, bearing right to rejoin Main Street.

The Worth & Sladen valleys

Distance: 4½ miles (7km). Time: 2½ hours
Terrain: Mainly field paths, some tracks. A relatively strenuous walk with a
moderate and a fairly steep climb, a number of stiles and some wet areas
and tricky path finding – boots are essential.
Start: Haworth Tourist Information Centre, grid ref 030373.
Parking: Good choice of car parks in Haworth village.
Refreshment/facilities: Excellent choice in Haworth. Toilets near Parsonage.
Public Transport: Frequent buses 500, 664, 665 from Keighley (500 from
Hebden Bridge Station) plus Keighley Worth Valley trains to Haworth at
weekends and school holidays

*This is a particularly attractive walk, exploring and crossing two of the three
Pennine tributary valleys of Airedale above which Haworth is situated.
There are some very attractive riverside sections, paved paths and unspoiled
Pennine scenery – quiet landscapes that offer a contrast to the bustling
tourist centre of Haworth.*

From Haworth Tourist Information Centre walk up West Lane, to the left of
the Old White Lion Inn. Where it meets the main road, North Street, cross,
and turn sharp right for 80 yards to where a track signed 'Public Footpath
private road' on the left leads past Currer House. This becomes a green track
enclosed between walls and an open field. Keep on through the stile by the
gate ahead, as the path descends the hillside. At the next stile, head half-right
through two isolated gateposts. Follow the ruined wall to your right which
leads down to Lower Oldfield Farm. The path goes through a wooden
pedestrian gate into a narrow enclosed way leading outside the farm. Just
past the house take the ladder stile to your right. This path follows an ancient
sunken 'hollow way' between the remnants of stone walls descending to
Long Bridge, an old packhorse bridge (020375).

Cross, but where the path forks, take the right-hand path, following the
banks of the pretty River Worth downstream. This is a lovely path, through
a typical Pennine valley, muddy in places, marked by ladder-stiles. Take the
ladder-stile in the wall on the right (025377) which takes you along the
riverside path to more stiles. At the next stile where the handsome Lord
Bridge carrying the road over the River Worth comes into view (027378),
your route is sharp left, following the wall uphill to where, across a track,
you see a kissing-gate stile ahead. Go through this, alongside the wall to
reach stone steps which take you towards large farm buildings above. To the

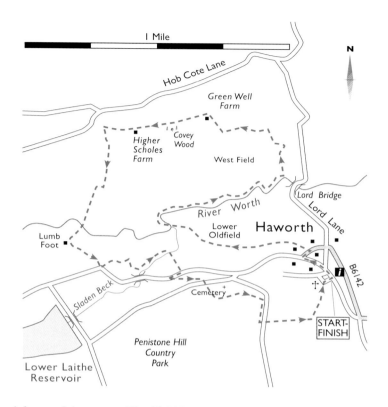

left a gate brings you to West Field Farm.

Turn right in the track, but go left beside and behind the farm to where you will see, on the right, a stile. Go over this up to another stile and follow the path alongside the wall to a stile in the wall corner ahead (026381). Go through here then sharp left to follow the wall side to the next stile in the wall ahead. Bear half right up the hillside to where, in the corner of a ruined wall above, you will see a ruined stile. Follow the next wall to the left to where a stile and gate lead to an enclosed track to Green Well Farm.

Go through the gate and to the right of the farm, and along the farm access track. Where this swings around a hairpin bend, look for the remains of a stile in the wall corner which gives access to a path that contours the hillside leading to Covey Wood where a bench provides a perfect picnic spot.

This is an especially beautiful little wood, with splendid views across to Haworth village, to Penistone Hill Country Park and the summits of the

11

South Pennines watershed beyond. Covey Wood with its oak and pine trees, wildflowers and pond, was planted in 2000 by fifty-eight members of the Covey Family, in memory of Eva Covey and her husband Bert.

From Covey Wood continue in the same direction through stiles, keeping directly ahead to a complex of buildings known as Higher Scholes. A stile to the right of the farm leads to a path behind the buildings. Keep ahead past cottages to the farm drive. At the lane, cross and take the path over the stile opposite, but bear half-right to a half-hidden stone stile in the wall ahead. Keep ahead to a wire gate by stone steps leading into a farm track (016382). Left here, through the farmyard to the field gate below. Your path now follows long-vanished walls by the side of a narrow gill. Descend to meet and cross a green track, Hey Lane (016377). Turn right, over the stile, but where the path forks, take the left fork along a paved path continuing down the gill. This eventually emerges at another attractive packhorse bridge below Lumb Foot.

Follow the lane uphill through the hamlet of Lumb Foot, the start of a long steep climb, as it twists up to Stanbury Road. Turn left, with the footpath sign, immediately before reaching the road, to follow a quiet track past Milking Hill Farm. The right of way goes past the farm and into the farmyard – keep right past the sheep pens to the metal gate which leads to a wallside path which descends to the Sladen Beck at a ladder stile near Sladen Bridge (018372). Turn left along the track into the valley towards cottages. Before these, a sign indicates a path to the right over Sladen Beck at a grass covered bridge leading to stone steps. Climb these, then follow the field edge to emerge on Sun Lane.

Turn right for 80 yards to where a signpost indicates three paths heading up and over the moor. Take the most easterly of these, signed Urban Common. This is a narrow not easily visible path, no more than a narrow hollow through heather and bilberry as it heads diagonally and very steeply up the hillside to emerge at Cemetery Road close to Haworth. Turn left here but after 80 yards on the right, by picnic tables, a path (signed) leads onto the moor. Take the right fork which follows Haworth Cemetery Wall – another steep ascent – into Penistone Hill Country Park.

About 120 yards from the cemetery wall corner, past a mound of heather, (024370) a path heads off to the left. Take this one, as it offers more fine views across the Sladen and Worth Valleys and Haworth itself, as it curves past old quarry workings to join the lane. Before the lane take the grassy path right, parallel to the road, to reach the junction of paths into Penistone Hill and a small parking area (027371). Cross the lane to the footpath sign that indicates the track to Haworth along Balcony Lane. Take this track as it descends to the village, turning left at the junction along the paved path by a car park, hen runs and graveyard, to emerge in Main Street.

Top Withins

Distance: 6 miles (9.5km). Time: 3 hours
Terrain: Tracks, moorland paths and lane; one long and one shorter climb.
Start: Penistone Hill Country Park Grove Hill car park (018363), or Stanbury.
Parking: Small public car park in SW corner of Penistone Hill Country Park
(018363). Alternative car parks in Country Park close by.
Refreshment/facilities: Friendly Inn and Wuthering Heights pub, Stanbury.
Toilets 50 metres south of car park on Moor Lane (alternative car park).
Public Transport: Bus 664 from Keighley to Stanbury (not Sundays).
Limited service 918 to Stanbury Sundays. Summer Sunday/BHs 812 from
Keighley/Haworth passes walk start at Penistone Hill.

This is the classic and popular Brontë walk following the footsteps of the sisters to Brontë Falls then climbing up the little valley of South Dean Beck to the iconic ruined farm of Top Withins. The return walk to the Pennine village of Stanbury offers splendid views over Lower Laithe Reservoir.

From the car park, cross Moor Side Lane and follow the well-signed path (Millennium Way) due westwards across the moorland. This path gradually descends to join the main Brontë Way track below at Lower Intake – it can be wet and muddy in places, so when wet the lower track can be used. Continue along the brow of the hill down into the Gill to Brontë Falls.

This little waterfall is described in both letters and poems by Emily and Charlotte as one of their favourite walks from the Parsonage. With Top Withins, it is a key place of pilgrimage for Brontë worshippers worldwide.

Follow the path steeply up the hillside, heading up gritstone steps to a kissing gate. At the junction (998360), your path is sharp left heading below fields through a gap stile. Keep ahead in a broad field towards a ladder-stile. The path now starts the long ascent, winding up across open moorland up the shoulder of the little valley, soon fording a shallow stream at stepping stones. The ruined farm building and sole sycamore tree is your destination ahead. It is a steady climb, past the junction with the Stanbury path, and then a final pull to the summit at Top Withins.

The location of this old farmhouse was a likely inspiration for the Earnshaw's home of Wuthering Heights, though the building described in the book was almost certainly inspired by local Elizabethan and Jacobean farmhouses. A plaque on the far wall explains the literary connections. With its solitary tree, this evocative ruin is now world-famous. It also offers

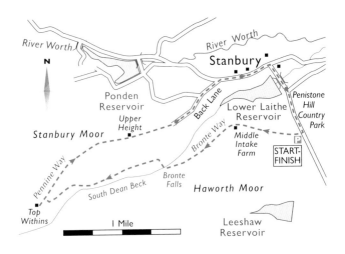

magnificent views into the Worth Valley, Airedale and beyond.

You are now on the Pennine Way. Return the way you came, downhill for 200 yards, before forking left with the Pennine Way along a narrow path which gently contours then descends the hillside past the ruins of Lower Within, before becoming a track which skirts the hillside then ascends a low knoll. Keep straight ahead with the signs towards Stanbury as the track broadens as it reaches Upper Heights. Take the left fork here, again keeping due east with the Stanbury signs where the Pennine Way bears off north-wards, sharp left. The main track descends to a metal gate at a junction of paths leaving the open access area – with views of Lower Laithe Reservoir as you descend. This eventually becomes a tarmac lane, Back Lane, which emerges at the bus stop turning circle at the west end of Stanbury village.

Stanbury is a typical Pennine linear hill village, with a Victorian school, two inns, and several attractive eighteenth- and nineteenth-century cottages and barns. The village once housed workers from outlying farms and the long vanished water-powered wool and cotton mills on the valley floor.

From Stanbury follow the main road, before turning right 200 yards below the village to follow the lane (keeping right to face traffic) across the dam of Lower Laithe Reservoir. Unless you are returning to Haworth (if so take the first track left which leads towards the village) continue straight ahead – there is a pavement on the left and, as you approach Pennine Hill Country Park, an elevated grassy verge path leading uphill to the car park.

Ponden Hall

Distance: 6 miles (9.5km). Time: 2½ hours
Terrain: **Tracks** and moorland paths; one fairly steep climb, some areas of boggy moorland – boots essential.
Start: Stanbury village centre, grid ref 011371.
Parking: **Limited** parking in Stanbury – avoid yellow lines and narrow street **section**. NB Please do not risk damage by parking or obstructing **turning** circle at Hob Hill as this is used by large buses.
Refreshment/facilities: Friendly Inn and Wuthering Heights pub, Stanbury.
Toilets: **50 yards** south of car park on Moor Lane, Penistone Hill, ½ mile.
Public Transport: Bus 664 from Keighley via Haworth, hourly, weekdays, limited **Sunday** service 918; also service 812 June to end of August only.

This walk from the typical Pennine village of Stanbury enjoys a short but scenic section of the Pennine Way. It crosses the Upper Worth Valley, passing old farms, Ponden Reservoir and Ponden Hall, taking a steep climb up to Oakworth Moor and returning along a high level route via Oldfield.

Walk through Stanbury village to Hob Hill (005370) – bus users alight here – bearing left up Back Lane, turning first right towards Cold Knoll Farm. Keep ahead here, but at the next junction, Buckley Green (998367), take the right fork with the Pennine Way signs, descending a track towards Buckley Farm, keeping right at a gate down a grassy walled track to Rush Isles to join a tarmac lane. Turn left here, and walk alongside the lower edge of Ponden Reservoir. Bear right up to handsome Ponden Farm with its 1689 date stone.

Many people have suggested that this lovely old seventeenth century farmhouse was the inspiration for Thrushcross Grange in Wuthering Heights. Though the location is appropriate, the novel depicts a large, grander mansion reflecting the Linton family's manufacturing wealth.

Cotton grass – a common feature of boggy moorland.

Follow the track uphill past the junction, keeping ahead to go to the left of and above Whitestone

15

Denholme and Thornton, with the city of Bradford in its shallow valley beyond.

After about a quarter of a mile, on the brow of the hill at 047329 (*not* as shown on the OS map), a kissing-gate in the fence, right, leads to a path which follows the edge of the moor. It climbs steadily, with ever more spectacular views across the industrial Worth Valley with a backcloth of wild fells beyond.

Follow the paths for over a mile, through old quarry workings, heading for the little cairn high on Nab Hill. The great line of turbines on Ovenden Moor increasingly dominates views to the south.

There is a small stone refuge here, with breathtaking views in every direction. Descend slightly to pick up an old quarry track which eventually emerges on Nab Water Lane just north of Ovenden Moor. Turn right here, downhill, but after 120 yards a stile on the right leads to another moorland path, this time below Nab Scar. Follow the narrow path through rough moorland grass straight ahead, soon following the ruined walls of a path enclosure. Where this ends (033328), look for a pedestrian gate in the fence below, left. The path follows the remains of a wall downhill bearing left to the gate and crossing a drain at a bridge before a second gate into the lane.

Go right here for 25 yards then through a wooden pedestrian gate on the left. Just past some old enclosures, the path joins and follows a catchwater drain. As you approach a field gate, bear right across the moorland towards a small, newish pedestrian gate which leads back into the lane.

Turn left and walk for another quarter of a mile, as the lane dips across a narrow gill, towards a mobile phone mast, then take the path right (signed) (029337), just beyond the bridge over the gill. This path follows a wire fence downhill. Head for the metal pedestrian gate in the wall below and continue to where a stone bridge, right, crosses the gill. Cross, the path now heading through a shallow gulley. Head towards the farmhouse below (waymarked), going through a metal gate onto the farm drive to join a track past houses and stables, contouring the hillside. At the last house, look for a narrow, sunken path, right, by a cypress tree (032344). This old and lovely way curves below farm buildings, between walls, becoming a track past cottages, emerging in Oxenhope along Hill House Lane. Turn right into Low Town for bus stop and post office.

Newsholme Dean & Goose Eye

Distance: 4 miles (6km). Time: 2 hours
Terrain: Track, field paths and short sections of lane. One short and one longer and quite steep climb, and a couple of awkward stiles.
Start: Laycock chapel/bus terminus, grid ref 033410.
Parking: Roadside parking in Laycock on broad section of Laycock Lane.
NO parking in Goose Eye. Turkey Inn car park strictly for pub patrons.
Refreshment/facilities: None in Laycock. Turkey Inn in Goose Eye.
No toilets except for pub (patrons only). Nearest Keighley.
Public Transport: Bus 710 from Keighley to Laycock every 30 minutes weekdays, hourly Sundays.

This short, but especially lovely walk, uses some delightful footpaths through woodland and past mill ponds, following Dean Beck, a tributary valley of the River Worth, to Newsholme Dean. Until the middle of the last century, Newsholme Dean was a popular beauty spot and picnic area where generations of people from industrial Keighley went for a walk on Sunday afternoons.

From the bus terminus or village hall in the centre of Laycock, continue along Laycock Lane heading westwards, past the Goose Eye road junction towards Sutton and Cross Hills. At the next fork bear left along Totley Hall Road, but almost immediately take the (signed) path through the gap stile left. Descend steps and follow the wall to the next gap stile below into a steep gill.

Ignore sheep paths to the left, making your way down the steep side of the clough (027407), crossing the stream at rough stepping stones (tricky after rain). Ignore the stile opposite by keeping left, downstream, to a tall Millennium Way wooden signpost. Follow the path along the stream side to where it meets a track. Bear left here into the centre of Goose Eye hamlet.

Goose Eye probably takes its name

*Woodland flowers:
primroses and violets.*

27

from 'Goose Hey' – a field where geese were kept, but the hamlet grew around two eighteenth-century cotton mills powered by water from Dean Beck. One of the mills, Turkey Mill, gave its name to the popular Turkey Inn, a pub which welcomes walkers with muddy boots – and even wet dogs – with food and real ale. Goose Eye is also the name of a popular local real ale, once brewed near the pub but now in nearby Keighley. Toilets available for pub patrons only.

From Goose Eye, turn right and follow the lane through the hamlet, for 100 yards, uphill, to where on the right, a gap stile and steps lead to a footbridge. Cross, following the stream and going over the next footbridge over the mill race, and into a lovely wooded valley, passing a waterfall. Where the path forks keep to the right, north of the large mill pond. Keep right again at the next fork, ascending the higher path, through oak and alder woods. This eventually joins a wider path and becomes a paved track which climbs to join a track into the hamlet of Newsholme Dean. Turn left here, past cottages, keeping left at the fork (signed Newsholme) along the track which descends into the valley of Newsholme Dean, curving left over the handsome hump-backed bridge. Keep straight ahead across the valley floor with the bridlepath waymarks, heading for the gate which leads to the very steep path through the woods of Newsholme Dean.

The word 'dean' means wooded valley in old English, and this pretty wooded hillside of oak and alder is typically Pennine in character. Bill O' th' Hoylus End (otherwise known as William Wright), a once well-known local Victorian dialect poet, celebrated a pretty farm girl he met here with his poem The Lass o' Newsholme Dean.

Climb through and past the wood, at the top of which the path veers slightly left towards a gate in the wall above. Climb up to and through the gate (019401), which leads into a farm track. Keep ahead to reach the farm at Newsholme. Follow the main track slightly to the right as it twists between farm buildings through the hamlet of Newsholme that used to have a chapel – but still has a post box.

Walk 120 yards along the lane south of the village before turning left into a narrow lane in front of farm buildings. Follow this lane as it becomes an unsurfaced track.

There are fine views from here across to Oakworth Cemetery – the houses just visible on the horizon are the outskirts of Oakworth (Walk 6).

Continue past Low Laithe Farm; where the track descends and curves right, look for a narrow gap-stile on the left of the bend (027400) which leads through a small enclosure into a field. Follow the wall downhill, to where the path curves left above Spring Well Gill to a gap stile into a farm access road. Turn right here into the lane.

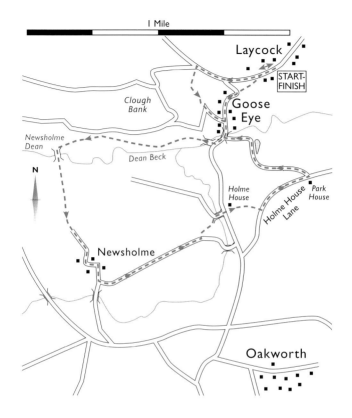

Take the path (signed) almost directly opposite which follows a track by a wall, then across two fields. Keep the same direction as the path dips and climb to join Holme Lane at a stile. Turn left here keeping on the left hand side on the outside of the bend to avoid speeding traffic. Where a lovely old cobbled lane angles in from the left opposite Park House (034403), turn sharp left to follow this lane as it descends back into the Newsholme Valley, past a small mill pond, emerging just to the west of Goose Eye. Walk through the hamlet, keeping on narrow pavements to avoid traffic, but at the last bend (029408) go through the gap-stile, right, to join a flagged path which climbs steeply up the hillside (fine views) past cottages, becoming Robert Street into the centre of Laycock.

Worth Valley Railway walk

Distance: 5½ miles (9km). Time: 3 hours
Terrain: Tracks, field paths, one climb, a few steep sections and awkward stiles.
Start: Keighley Railway Station, grid ref 065413.
Parking: Public car parks in Keighley – alternative is to use the free station
car park at Oxenhope, take train to Keighley and walk back to car.
Refreshment/facilities: Keighley and Oxenhope Station (when railway
open). Pub, shop in Oxenhope.
Public Transport: Frequent trains and buses to Keighley; railway station 5
mins walk from bus station. Return from Oxenhope by a Worth Valley train
(weekends and holidays) or catch 500 bus from station, or bus 720 from
the top of Station Road – cross to bus stop on Denholme Road ahead.

*This walk follows mostly well waymarked paths parallel to the famous
Worth Valley Steam Railway, with some spectacular views of steam trains at
weekends through the Worth and Bridgehouse Beck valleys. In the central
section of the walk the route leaves river and railway to give panoramic
views above Hainworth and below Haworth Brow.*

From the front of Keighley Station turn left towards the town then first left
down cobbled Low Mill Lane. After 200 yards, as the lane bends right, look
across to where a narrow alleyway leads between high walls, waymarked
Worth Way. This leads to an atmospheric urban path, a little intimidating at
first, below the railway line and past old factories. Keep with the Worth Way
as it turns right over a footbridge and under a short tunnel into Coney Lane.

*Notice the tall stone chimney in front of the derelict factory on the right with
its 'stone head' complete with a bowler hat carved in the stonework.*

Cross the lane, continuing with the Worth Way between railway and
builder's yard. The path soon opens up into attractive woodland alongside
the River Worth.

You reach Victoria Road – ahead are the warehouses of Timothy Taylor's
Brewery at Spring Bank where the famous Landlord Ale is brewed.
Follow the road left over the railway bridge to the junction with
Hainworth Wood Road.

Cross into Woodhouse Road, climbing past a small estate of houses behind
which, on the right (062399), an unsurfaced track (marked Aire-Calder link)
climbs steadily through Hainworth Wood. Continue uphill until you pass
Nether House to emerge on Hainworth Lane. Turn left up to Hainworth.

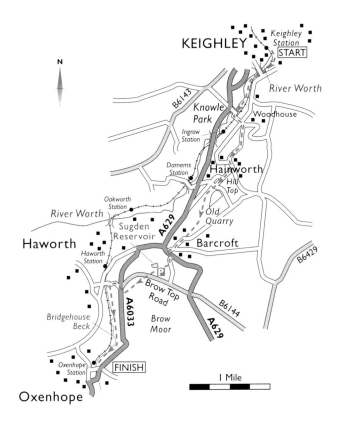

You may be a little more than a mile from Keighley town centre, but Hainworth is an unspoiled rural hamlet, with typical South Pennines eighteenth- and nineteenth-century cottages and fine views to the west.

Turn right in the village centre along Hill Top Lane (with Worth Way signs). Follow the track to another cluster of cottages at Hill Top, where you take the left fork, with the Worth Way signs, to follow what becomes a beautiful path below an old quarry, past heather and bilberry, with panoramic views across the valley.

Follow this path for a mile until it joins Bingley Road, descending into the hamlet of Barcroft above Cross Roads. Just past the 30mph sign (047376) take the signed path left but, after 20 yards, at a junction, take the lower path right, marked Senior Way, leading into a narrow walled section, right, to join

31

the lane. Turn left here, left again at the fork down to the main A629 Denholme Road. Cross with care, but just to the right is the start of a track, Hardgate Lane (047375), which soon zigzags right then left before curving up to more cottages. Almost opposite these look for a stone step-stile on the right that leads to a faint path alongside a wall. This contours the hillside above a shallow ravine. Keep ahead above Sugden Reservoir, following the wire fence alongside a small enclosure, towards the mobile phone mast ahead, to emerge at a car park. Continue to the entrance where a stile on the right leads into Haworth Brow Road.

Right here, but just by the 30mph sign, take the path left which skirts the edge of Haworth Brow Moor, through heather and moorland grass, heading towards a cottage at the lane. Turn left here, but almost immediately cross to the area of grassland. Below the bench, follow a path which descends to the junction with the main Hebden Road. Cross and continue steeply down Brow Road. At the bottom corner, where the road bends sharp right into Haworth (036369), take the path left, signed Oxenhope. This leads up steps and along an enclosed way between fences. Follow the main path through pedestrian gates and stiles, alongside Bridgehouse Beck, bridging and then following the embankment of an abandoned mill race, before climbing up in front of a house (037362).

Just beyond the patio take the waymarked path right, down to, then alongside, the stream. Ignore a tempting stone arch bridge but cross the next footbridge (037358) to reach the drive to North Ives Barn. Continue past the sewage works, beyond the entrance to which a narrow path continues by the stream. Cross the next footbridge then walk alongside the stream, over a headland (ignoring the next bridge) finally to emerge behind the carriage sheds of Oxenhope Station. Turn right for the station – the 500 bus stop is directly opposite, and the 720 stop is at the top of Station Road.